Silent Whispers, Loud Callings

Purnima J.

BookLeaf Publishing
India | USA | UK

Made with ❤ on the BookLeaf Publishing Platform
www.bookleafpub.in
www.bookleafpub.com

Dedication

Well there are some who takes you on a journey
And there are some who shapes your journey
Then there are some who makes your journey
Also there are some who breaks your journey
But
All are with a certain goal
All are here to play their role

So, to all of you who have been a part of my journey
Be it my family, my friends or any enemy
I feel grateful to you for shaping my life
And hopeful that you all have/lead a good life

"Lovingly dedicated to my beloved instant, constant and distant family"

Preface

It's an outpour of emotions by a fairly simple introvert.

-Barely serious, Mostly fun

This collection of poems is a reflection of the silent world within an introvert's heart. It is the result of years spent observing, feeling, and absorbing the world from the shadows of solitude. In each verse, there is a story—often quiet, sometimes overwhelming—that is drawn from the depths of personal experience and emotion.

What you hold in your hands is not merely a collection of words, but a piece of an ongoing journey—an exploration of what it means to live, to be alone, and yet to feel deeply connected to the world in ways that words cannot fully capture. Through these poems, I hope to share the beauty of quiet introspection and the power of vulnerability in a world that often celebrates noise over stillness. This book is for anyone who has ever felt the weight of emotions they couldn't easily express, for those who have found solace in silence, and for anyone seeking a voice in the spaces between words.

Acknowledgements

I would like to extend my heartfelt gratitude to everyone who has supported me on this quiet journey of writing. As an introvert, I often find my thoughts louder than words, and my world larger in silence than in speech. This book is a reflection of those inner landscapes, and while I may not always have voiced my gratitude aloud, I carry it deeply in my heart.

To my family and friends, thank you for your understanding and patience. You have allowed me the space to grow within myself, and for that, I am forever grateful. Your support has been both an anchor and a gentle push, helping me believe that what is shared in solitude can still be meaningful to others.

Monday Night

There was a full moon sight
On a cool Monday night
And pop came she out
Much to her parents' delight

She was long overdue
To make her debut
Was it the world that she feared
Or was she just lazy, who knew

I bet she had a good time
Unbothered, yet cuddled in slime
That abode was her haven
She wouldn't trade it for a dime

But she had no choice
They were all deaf to her voice
She had stalled it for long
It was their turn to rejoice

That's when she saw the beam
Peeping through the bloodstream
She knew it was almost time
To meet them and scream

There was this cool Monday night
Full moon was in sight
When pop came she out
Much to her folks' delight

Early Days

Bittersweet memories of my early childhood
Came flooding back to me
The flashes were mostly blurry
But the feeling still crystal clear to me

The baby-walker gave me immense freedom
To gobble up mud at a lightning speed
Chewing on clay and chalk was so normal
But sneakily sipping on their leftover tea was a steal

As much as the mind was curious
About everything that came my way
I got fascinated by every insect, frog and crawler
Just like the mysteries of night and day

I was as fond of swings and slides
As I was keen to primp our baby hound
The towering stature of eucalyptus gave me nightmares
Whilst the wiggle of an earthworm was too profound

Mom's makeup and jewels were a fascination
Always loved that pair of cute white heels
Coloured nails and smooth hair often caught my eye
But rings and anklets for me were the real deal

Veggies for me were a big no no
Never liked going near mustard fields
Applying kohl always brought me tears
While facing darkness I had to put forth my shield

Going down the memory lane
Brought back bittersweet memories
The carefree days of early childhood
Sure made me nostalgic, but no worries

No Escape

Sitting by the window pane
While loneliness driving her insane
The quiet little girl often wondered
How everything around her got so twisted
And to whom does she complain

She must have been all of six
When life tossed its first challenge at her
Oblivious to what was forthcoming
Her mind wrestled to clear away the blur

By the time it all began to make some sense
Her anchor got steered away from her
Struggling as he was to keep pace at boarding school
This little girl started feeling the absence of her big
brother

Baffled by her father's decision
To send her brother far away
Unable to fathom a plausible explanation
She felt as if trickery was at play

She always loved being around her brother
Felt so happy, relaxed and carefree

He would often take the fall for her shortcomings
There was nothing she asked and he wouldn't agree

It was all going fine until the day
He was decided to be sent away
This was her first of many setbacks
And eventually she lost her track

Her mother was completely inconsolable
As her heart ached with rage
Unwilling to come to terms yet
How her son would manage everything at such a tender
age

She would often stay cold and depressed
Being indifferent to the ones around
The atmosphere at home was mostly grim
Once the doting mom was hardly to be found

The sweet boy too was in a state of complete disbelief
For once he felt relieved only to be left shattered
The reality to him was nothing short of a nightmare
But prudent sure he was to have agreed to what
mattered

Mistaking it for being easier than to deal with
The quintessential good boy settled against his will

Little did he know the scoldings were nothing as compared
Life there was a race, whereas here he could chill

Her father held onto his decision
Absolutely nothing could alter his conviction
He knew what was best for his son
Despite being opposed and inviting friction

No, it wasn't easy for any of them
To accept what altered their course of being
But the plunge had long been taken
So, there was no looking back or fleeing

SUNDAY

SUNDAY, the universal funday, resonated with me
deeply
So much so that as a child, I associated mine with HOLI
We used to wake up to the aroma of something special
For taking a shower in the morning, there was no hustle
There used to be a lot of fun and frolic that day
Everybody would be in a mood to relax, enjoy and play

On the table would lay our favourite spread
There would be no one scolding, whom we dreaded
Either there would be friends coming over
Or we would go out to meet someone there

Mornings, usually, would have a lazy start
But evenings would offer the best part
The sounds of laughter would echo in the halls
The colours of TV would light up the walls

The gaming sessions would be longer than usual
For movie outings we would prefer to wear casuals
We would all be drenched in the fervour of the day
It would feel, as if, our favourite HOLI was at play

Peace Within

They called me one day
To ask if I was doing ok
I said I have never been better
'Being at home' is what actually matters

But isn't home there where heart is
And your heart is there where art is
Well I could sit and appreciate art all day
But being closer to the family makes my heart sway

Happiness, however, is just a state of mind
Might get buried ten feet under, but still stay kind
Peace of mind, for me, always goes a long way
Away from all nonsense, just need a quiet day

Even little chaos around guests could be overwhelming
A secluded place in the meadows would be my thing
I would sit by the stream, working on my art
A life such as that would always have my heart

When the Sea fell in love with the Moon

Let me tell you a sob love story
It's from when the moon was in full glory
The sea was playful and in her bloom
She got smitten by him and began to croon

The moon seemed so fair and bright
The sea was enamoured by his might
She would eagerly await the night
Only to catch a glimpse of his sight

She would be elated and blush with delight
As and when she saw her mighty knight
She would jump and spin and happily dance
Whenever she found the golden chance

The moon too would have a glance
Maintaining his static poised stance
He knew he couldn't go any near
Even though he loved and cared

He would not make any advance
Since there was no room for romance
Their union would only cause uproar and stir

The situation would get chaotic and create a complete
blur

The moon was stationed outside the earth
He was tasked with protecting her worth
He appreciated his mission way too well
There was no recourse for him but to repel

The sea would not accept no for a reply
She was totally invested in the guy
She tossed, screamed and followed him across
Her anguish caused catastrophe and chaos

The whole world panicked as it was left stranded
Mother Nature intervened and promptly commanded
She jolted the sea and brought her back to senses
Despite sulking, she was prepared for the consequences

Mother Nature empathised with her emotion
As impressed she was by the moon's devotion
She let the moon visit his lady briefly
Even now upon his arrival, the sea swells swiftly

She rejoices, brightens up and behaves
As the moon loves to dance on her waves
Their love story might not seem perfect
But they both share a lot of affection and respect

Inner World

Everyday I see a little girl
Frolicking in the luscious meadows
Along comes a playful puppy
Following her like a shadow

She reaches out to the chipmunks
Searching for some luscious nuts
They swap it for some gentle caress
From the girl in the peasant dress

Pink cherry blossoms by the stream
Is next as a part of her scheme
She paces there to fetch the blooms
The perfect antidote to wipe out the gloom

Her next expedition is to meet the bees
Their honey makes for the perfect recipe
She seems to have formed some affinity
Or do they mistake her for divinity?

Those long golden locks get butterflies cheering
I wonder what makes her so endearing
Is it her calm demeanour that is so reassuring
Or is it the fact that she is so gentle and caring?

She heads back home after a fulfilling day
The birds fly along as if clearing her pathway
Her heart seems as full as her basket is
What she does with her riches remains a quiz

The Shadow and The Strength

As the darkness of night drags her veil
And evil forces crawl out to play
A mysterious shadow follows him around
To control his path everyday

She leads him to a life of filth and disgrace
He has nowhere to go but to drag himself through this phase
His situation is grim but he's not miscreant
He's not frightened of her but can't break the restraints

He's stuck with her for eternity
She won't let him live with dignity
She's got a hold of his body and mind
He's struggling for the life he's left behind

No, he ain't one who you can easily suppress
But off late he's been under a lot of duress
She puts him up for tasks he strongly reprehends
And sends him off to alleys even she wouldn't dare comprehend

Oh she's cold as a witch, wicked are her ways

But it's his pious soul that she can't set ablaze
She's relentlessly trying to shatter his resolve
But a calm demeanour is what he has evolved

He remains unperturbed by her malicious plots
Violent with rage she tosses him afar to rot
Such an opportunity is what he's long been waiting for
He jumps right at it and escapes out the front door

No, it hasn't been as easy as it might seem
He couldn't have left her to ruin others' dreams
She has been feeding herself on torture and torment
He made sure to stay placid and coaxed her to repent

The Unbreakable Bond

She shared her love with you, my dear
It wasn't easy for her, to be clear
It's not a fault that you are here
We wished for it that you would appear

She jumped at the idea of you being here
It was endearing for her to have a sibling so near
But you would need a lot of love and care, is what she
feared
This realisation made her excitement soon disappear

She feared you would come and dethrone her
Your presence is what she would have to deter
Sensing her fear, we had to assure her,
"This is not a competition and there is no heir
You are the first born, our precious one
She will magnify the love, it will be more fun
You'll share a close bond like no other
She'll keep your secrets safe from all others
You might not always agree, but it won't matter
You both will still go strong, if you just have each other"

She somehow made her peace with it
But she still wasn't sure how she'd deal with it

She made us promise we'll never forget her
She's not a choice, we wouldn't detest her

It's not like we prefer one over the other
You both are precious, both are equally dear
If one is the heart, other is it's beat
Can't live without you both, we say that on repeat

Pure Indulgence

Drooling over the lip-smacking delectable
With my eyes set on the exceptional eatable
I stand right across the shelf of my favourite find
And patiently wait for my dad to read through my mind

One can totally rely on it when things go blurry
You can partake some of it in a state of worry
Could be the ideal gift when you are in a hurry
Proves sinful every time after having that spicy curry

It wiggles your mind and touches your soul
It energises you when you dwindle away from the goal
It's comforting when sulking alone post breakup
If hesitant to talk, it could be the deal-breaker

Seems impossible to sneakily open its wrapper in
another room,
Forget others, the child at home will certainly fume
If you snatch it from someone, they'll throw a fit
Stealing it is a crime, they'll happily commit

If you know what I meant then honestly confess
Isn't a bar of chocolate pure bliss, if no less
It isn't just another sweet, it's an indulgence

It's a symbol of prestige in every sense

It wields the authority to engage all five senses
It certainly is one of your life's best expenses
It's like a prized possession one sure does envy
You have to earn it every time, doesn't come
easily

First Quinquennium

I hopped, skipped and jumped
To my first five-year leap
My journey has been enthralling
Riding carefree on toy cars and jeeps

Fresh breeze and mighty thunder
Mild dew and bright Sun yonder
Starry skies and rainbow glee
All these still blow my mind with queries

It's been a trip from liking blue to yellow
Marching ahead from being wild to mellow
Rattles and lullabies are now a thing of the past
The story-reading sessions are now more advanced

The 'world of hues' has always brought delight to me
But playing bat-ball is the new respite for me
Both young and old have been kind to me
I'm the star of my family unanimously

My experiences so far have been pleasing
I hope showers of your blessings are never ceasing
So, here I pray for all of you to stay
And wish me love and luck on my fifth birthday

Another Year Another Story

See how soon time flies by...
It's the same day
Yet another starry sky
Our baby has grown by leaps and bounds,
As if with just a blink of an eye.

Each day brought with it new excitement
For you, for him and for the distant eyes
Excited were you
Admiring the innocent mischiefs
Excited was he
Unfolding the childhood surprises
Excited were we
Cherishing the weekly goodbyes

The laughter, the giggle, the baby-talk
We admire his tiny-mini walk
His response to music is artless and instant
The spins appear as dance from a distance

Let's add to the cart of everlasting memories
Yet another bundle of joy
While showering on our baby warm wishes
As we celebrate his second birthday

Butterfly Flutterby

Fly fly my butterfly
Fly up high and touch the sky
Fly away far fly somewhere near
Fly till the stars seem closer and clear

Three deeply rooted years have gone by
It's time to break the cocoon and soar the skies
Ditch away thy slumber my flutterby
There's beauty beyond all this than what meets the eye

Blink thy eyes and spread thy wings
Widen thy horizon and dance to the music of springs
Smell some fragrant flowers
They have a lot to offer
Reveal thy true shades
And be one with the nature
Imbibe every delicate flavour
Draw their rich essence
Impart thy own fragrance
And make some true sense

Let the whole world behold thy real beauty
To ensure thy present thy best will be my duty
Tread on the sacred path of sharing and insight

Determine thy soul's hidden metal and might
Enrich thy life by allowing divine light
Pave thy path to success all glorious and bright

The New You

As the clock of your life cooed 'sixth'
I had a surge of emotions, all mixed
For one, you got the best gift of life ever
Also, you got termed 'the big one' forever

The long and exhausting wait finally got over
As we welcomed another of our angels come over
The union of you two has been a promise larger than life
To love, laugh, live and lead one another for life

Many a days, you have rushed straight to her
Just to catch a glimpse or simply gush about her
Beaming as you are during this phase in your life
Full of giggles, hugs, kisses and cuddles from a tiny new
life

Striving to strike a balance every single day
Somewhere down the line, we slipped away
Assuming our still small yet sensible girl will never go
astray
Our attention got divided to your utter dismay

Embroiled in all the chaos going around
Both you and I had our instances of a break down

At times it was you, unaware of when to pull the plug
Other times, I didn't realise all you needed was a warm
mommy-hug

Sadly the year gone by turned out a bit rough for you
Nonetheless we had our share of hearty laughter too
Unreal expectations from you turned you older for your
years
Your innocence got compromised far more than you
could bear

How I wish I could undo all that can't be undone
I wish I could bring back the days of endless fun
I remember we had our doubts about the forthcoming
change
And I had to give my word that nothing would be
estranged

All I can do now is make yet another promise
An assurance of the merriment that you would never
miss
What I would need in return, now that you are six
Is a little patience and understanding and that would do
the trick

But not for once let the negativity haunt you in any way
You will forever remain our charming princess any given

day
Always live your life to the fullest with arms wide open
Stay true to your new companion like the beach is to the
ocean

A Love That Lasts

Someone special somewhere is made just for you
But only time can tell where, how and who
You might feel allured to all the options lying for you out
there
But such are matters of the heart and your heart would
certainly become aware

Some might go crazy trying to figure it all out
When caring and sensing is what it's always about
Whether you wish to chase it or simply let it slide
It's bound to sweep you off your feet and leave you
mesmerised

We sure were in luck to be aware of it in time
Our hearts felt the connection as soon as the inner bells
chimed
We then embarked on our journey of uncertainties and
possibilities
What kept us going throughout was our undying love
and firm promises

Life always maintains a fine balance of kind versus cruel
If this moment feels ambiguous, next one everything
gets clear

We too had our share of upheavals and tranquility in life
Key being striking the perfect balance, came to us easy
with me being your wife

When one of us faltered somewhere, the other one
calmly stayed
We slayed the hardships together and gladly embraced
the accolades
We walked through our relationship with heads always
held up high
There wasn't too much in common, yet we found enough
reasons to joyously fly

Now we have knocked off several years, much to our
delight
It's been a fulfilling union with lots of affection and
occasional bouts of fight
Here's to a lifetime of togetherness while still coping
with each other
I wish you the happiest anniversary of love with
absolutely nothing to smother

Munchkin Turns Two

Hey mommy, look I'm only turning two
What else do you expect your little munchkin to do?
No mommy, don't just panic yet
I'm trying to give you moments you'll never forget

You know I like what you consider as waste
Mommy, sometimes I really doubt your taste
Your secret junkyard is an actual treasure
Watching you clean up after me gives me sheer pleasure

If you find me naughty, here I'm up for another mischief
If you feel I'm fussy, let me be your lil' chocolate thief
If my singing is what have you in splits
With my acting prowess, you'll barely spot the culprit
If my twists and twirls are what amaze you
How would you react to my big debut?
Does my wall art give you a headache?
Then my doodle on your face will surely keep you
awake

If at all you feel you are done with my outburst
It's my wailing that will give you jitters at first
I know I can still amuse you with my cute little capers
But walking in your heels is an assured dealbreaker

I have learnt how to make you rush towards me
Just don't loose control yet, you've a lot more to see
The lowest kitchen cabinet is my frequent hideaway
To grab and smudge your lipstick isn't just any child's
play

You look astound when I pick up a new word everyday
Yet my childhood antics are what you will miss one day
I know I do get on your nerves at times
With my made-up talks you are left speechless every
time

If my recent trips to the fridge are a call for worry
Consider yourself blessed as long as I don't spill the
curry
Since troubling you gives pleasure, I love to be your
prankster
After all to each of your wish and prayer, am I not the
only answer?

Whispers Of The Divine

That day He chose to answer all my prayers
And cajoled a tiny star to help end my despair
The star then happily obliged and descended upon my
way
You know that was five years ago on this very day

I then stumbled upon this very star
Which possessed the same charm quite as you
A closer look then clearly established
It was none other than my darling, you

My joy ever since knew no bounds
My heart pounding all the way through
For I had my dream in my arms
And that, my dear, happened to be you

Your tenderness magically soothed what was once a
barren land
Your glow possessed the magic to light up the tiniest
grain of sand
With a gleam of amusement you unfurled your mystic
world
To the tunes of which my whole and soul twirled

With you, days turned brighter and nights weighed
lighter
You kept on talking even if I went quieter
Months chased seasons while seasons rushed to years
You got me totally hooked when I lent you my ears

Life wouldn't be any merrier if it wasn't for you my dear
I wouldn't be who I am if neither of us were near
Your beauty took away my scars and smile wiped my
tears
Faith took over fears as I held you close all these years

It's been five years since, not even a sign of looking back
My life's running so swiftly as if it's on a fast-track
All this holds true for my dream is in my sight
And that my dear is you, my heart's true delight

I'll Forever Be With You

She beams with delight upon hearing her name
She holds me tight to overcome any fear or pain
She cuddles me by holding my face in her tiny hands
She expects me to follow her when no one else
understands
She looks for me when I am not seen around
She calls for me to help her climb down

I cherish the moment when I first saw her dimpled smile
I was in awe of her when I made her first hairstyle
I remember watching her when she first lifted her head
I was also there when she took her first baby step
The sound of her first mumble still echoes in my ears
I can't forget her first peck even to this year
I remember the nostalgia when she was first brought
home
And how amused I was when she first went out for her
roam
It was amazing to see her having her first hearty laugh
As much as it was endearing when she was given her
first bath

I have certainly been a part of many of her life's firsts

But what I wish for is to guide through all of her life's tests

34

Beyond The Dream

You are like a dream that really came true
Our precious little gem of the colour blue
You are our pleasure, you are our pride
You are a paradise, our own starry guide

Your aura is so angelic, a face so well defined
Your have a smile so pure so gentle and a heart so benign
Your embrace is so profound, could heal an ailing heart
Your kiss is so tender, could mend any torn out part

I fall short of words whenever I talk about you
Nonetheless I go on and on forever praising you
You are our little bundle of joy, the fodder for our sight
And you have actually made us 'King and Queen' in our
own right

That Was The Day

That was the day,
When he came into our lives,
And drove all the busy souls,
Out of their hives!

He was tender and small,
Cute as a bullet ball,
We were all enthralled,
But then he miauled,
As he was out of the caul!

That was the soft cry,
Which no wealth could buy,
We were high in the sky,
While he lay near by!

Today, he has grown tall,
And has started to crawl,
He is fair as a gaul,
But we still recall,
The day we heard the miaul!
That was the day.....

Love at first sight

While going through another casual survey
I noticed an unexpected picture on the display
I had been quite indifferent throughout the way
But that appearance had my mind blown away

I honestly couldn't believe what I had gazed
It took me a keen look to wipe out the haze
The image in front exceeded all expectations
In my heart I felt numerous intriguing sensations

I couldn't shake that image off my head
Overwhelmed that I was, everything went overhead
It was love at first sight, so to speak
Didn't have the heart to admit then, was too meek

I wasn't new to it, yet it felt so unique
It had a certain charm or should I say mystique
Can't really express how I felt at the time
I thought I was guilty of committing a crime

When it comes to love, I was already in my prime
I thought my admiration for her would last me a lifetime
Yet when I came across your tiny face initially
There was a strong connect almost instantly

There sure was divine presence in that cutest little face
Never thought I would have another surge of love at
such a fast pace

9 789369 545438